Fruit
from your
garden

For my family

Fruit
from your garden

Liz Brand

Illustrated by Rosemary Wise

THE NATIONAL TRUST

UNWIN HYMAN
London   Sydney

First published in Great Britain by Unwin
Hyman,
an imprint of Unwin Hyman Limited, 1987.

Published in association with The National Trust
for Places of Historic Interest or Natural Beauty.

UNWIN HYMAN LIMITED
Denmark House, 37–39 Queen Elizabeth Street
London SE1 2QB
and
40 Museum Street
London WC1A 1LU

Allen & Unwin Australia Pty Ltd
8 Napier Street, North Sydney, NSW 2060,
Australia

Allen & Unwin New Zealand Pty Ltd
with the Port Nicholson Press
60 Cambridge Terrace, Wellington, New Zealand

British Library cataloging in Publication Data
Brand, Elizabeth
  Fruit from your garden.
  1. Fruit-culture   2. Cookery (Fruit)
  I. Title   II. National Trust
  634   SB356

ISBN 0–04–440046–2

Designed by **Elizabeth Palmer**
Typeset by **Latimer Trend & Company Ltd,
Plymouth**
Printed in Great Britain by
William Clowes Ltd, Beccles & London

Contents

Introduction

There is an indefinable pleasure in harvesting home grown fruit which is totally out of proportion with such a natural and simple action. Indeed our involvement with the fruit's welfare is comparable to the concern of a fussing parent. The fruit tree is the pride of its nurturer, from its first few days in the ground, when it has to be lovingly sheltered

from winds, droughts and frosts, to its maturity when it bears plump, glowing, juicy fruit. Such are the emotions of the dedicated fruit grower. But whether we are such, or just enjoy pilfering the odd apple from a forsaken tree in the corner of the garden, there is no doubt that the satisfaction derived from this freshly picked bounty is one of the great joys of life.

Not surprisingly, every year the harvest will be declared to excel all past gleanings and to be incomparable to commercial produce. In purchasing fruit from the shop you also lose the thrill and excitement of sampling the very first fruit of the season. This pleasure is all too frequently denied by the availability of many fruits all year round, due to import and improved preservation techniques. The advantages of preservation must not be dismissed as the process avoids wastage when the inevitable glut occurs at peak season. So tips for each fruit are given whether it be for bottling, drying, freezing or making into jams, jellies or chutneys. Indeed there is nothing more rewarding and, less romantically, economical, than the satisfaction of surveying

rows of gleaming, rich conserves or plump, jarred fruit, all lovingly prepared and enjoying pride of place in the store cupboard.

Having extolled the mystic side of fruit growing, chance is not all-embracing. There are certain criteria over which mere mortals do have some control. Do, for example, choose a variety of plant which will be compatible with your soil-type and select a situation which is relatively frost free, sheltered and as sunny as possible. With careful planning, different varieties of fruit, such as strawberries, may be planted to ensure an extended season, thus prolonging the availability of fresh produce.

In the past there have been a far greater number of varieties to choose from, some peculiar to the selected areas where they flourish. Large-scale cultivation has streamlined the choice of strains but has also encouraged the emergence of improved and more resistant fruit. But for all the marvels of science, we are still able to enjoy hedgerow fruit, the wild hips, haws, blackberries, elderberries and sloes, which make excellent preserves, jellies, wines and sauces.

Apple and Crab Apple

(Malus family)

Despite being the most familiar fruit, the sight of an apple tree blossoming during spring and its boughs bending with ripened rosy fruit in the autumn, continues to delight. Apples are one of the oldest known fruits, myth recalls that one was the cause of man's initial downfall, its inviting appearance being too much to resist! Earliest fruits would have resembled wild crab apples *(Malus sylvestris)*, the first to be cultivated by man from which many varieties have been bred. The term 'costermonger' evolved from an early type of apple known as 'costard'. Sellers of these apples were nicknamed 'costard-mongers' and barrow fruit sellers have been called costermongers ever since.

Apple trees flourish in the temperate climate of the south and east on well drained soils. 'Cookers' may do better on nitrogen-rich soils than dessert apples and tolerate a higher rainfall. The trees should not be planted too close together

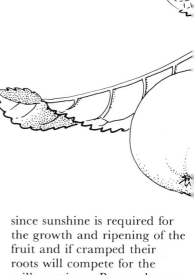

since sunshine is required for the growth and ripening of the fruit and if cramped their roots will compete for the soil's nutrients. But apple trees do require a certain amount of shelter to promote undisturbed pollination by insects and to protect the blossom from wind. A raised site is also preferable to guard against frost pockets, which are found in valleys and low lying regions and can damage the buds and blossom. A south-east facing slope is ideal.

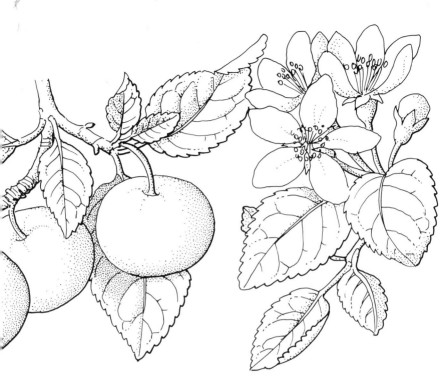

In early summer all those fruitlets which are likely to drop naturally will have done so, examine the branches and if they are still overburdened, thin out the fruitlets by hand. This will encourage the development of good quality fruit of even size and shape. The large centre apple of each cluster should be removed since it is usually mis-shapen.

Apples are ready for eating when the stalk comes away freely from the branch and the pips have ripened from white to brown. It is crucial to judge the right moment for picking if apples are to be stored since under-ripe fruit will shrivel and be bitter, and if over-ripe, will start decaying. Ideally the fruit should be mature, that is fully developed, not necessarily ripened. Any fruit which has been bruised through rough handling, or any 'windfalls' which have been picked up from the ground and are often insect ridden, should be used at once since they deteriorate quickly. Peel, core, remove damaged patches and use as desired. Choose blemish-free apples with the stalk still attached for storing. Wrap the apples individually in squares of newspaper for protection and to confine any rotting which may occur, to just one apple. Store in single layers and place so that they are not

shelf-life differs, early varieties such as 'Katy', 'Discovery' and 'James Grieve', should be eaten as soon as possible after picking, whereas the later varieties, 'Cox's Orange Pippin', 'Crispin' and 'Spartan', keep until after Christmas. The variety of apples available is so wide that there are endless combinations

'Russet'

touching, in a cool, dark place with a slightly moist atmosphere to prevent them turning woolly in texture or losing water and shrivelling. Generally, 'cookers' have a longer season and keep better than dessert apples. The

of colours, flavours and textures from the golden, dry 'Egremont Russet' to the crisp and juicy yellow 'Cox's Orange Pippin', splashed with red. Crab apples also offer a range of varieties from conical-shaped to almost

10

'Star Crimson'

'Granny Smith'

'Newton Wonder'

'Golden Delicious'

'Cox's Orange Pippin'

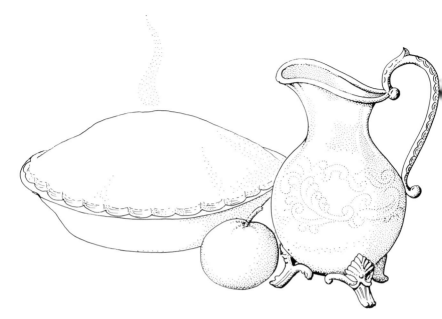

round fruits of yellow, orange, pink and red hues. Not all trees bear edible fruit, but of those which do 'John Downie', 'Transcendent' and 'Dartmouth' are amongst the favourites.

There are over six hundred varieties of apples in the United Kingdom and since only a handful are available through commercial sources, scope for the home grower to select a variety which has the characteristics to suit his or her purpose is almost endless. Most types are prone to disease; scab, canker, brown rot and silver leaf are the most

prevalent, and they also need protection against insects.

Apples provide the basis for many traditional puddings such as apple pie, strudel and crumble. Cored and baked in their skins with a little water and sugar, 'Bramley's Seedlings' are delicious served simply with custard. Stewed apple can be served similarly or used in charlottes, layered alternately with yoghurt and crushed ginger biscuits, or as a sauce to accompany pork. Coat sliced apples with fritter batter, use in muffins or combine with brown flour, sugar, spice and sultanas to make a farmhouse-style cake—windfalls are ideal for this.

Apples have a high pectin content which makes them excellent for jams, jellies and of course, apple butter. Their flavour is not particularly strong so they can be combined with other fruits which are low in pectin to give a better set without detracting from the fruit's flavour. Crab apples are traditionally made into a delicately flavoured, clear pink jelly, but where the subtle colour will not be appreciated, for instance when a mixture of fruit is used, then windfalls can equally well be substituted. Cider is made from fermented apple juice, the best quality being produced from true cider apples which are roughly categorised as sweets, bittersweets and sharps. If you have a glut of apples, try making homemade apple wine, if it's slightly cloudy, top up with soda water and add a sprig of mint for a long, refreshing drink.

The oldest method of preserving apples is by drying. Evidence of this can be traced back to the Stone Age when rings of apple were dried by the sun. Peel, core and slice into rings then dip in acidulated water, pat dry and string on to sticks, making sure the rings do not touch. Balance over a roasting tray and leave to dry as for figs (see page 38). When fully dried they should feel soft and rubbery. The dried fruit is delicious in compotes but can also be nibbled as a healthy snack. Apples are well suited to bottling—peel, core and slice into quarters, place in brine to prevent discoloration while you are doing so, then rinse and pack at once. Continue as for cherries (see page 23).

If the fruit is to be open frozen it should again be dipped in brine after slicing. Alternatively, freeze in sugar syrup to which a little ascorbic acid powder has been added. 'Cookers' are more suitable for freezing since dessert apples have a tendency to soften. Apple pulp is a useful standby and an excellent way of storing windfalls. Peel, core and cut out any blemishes. Simmer with a little water, cool, and freeze for up to six months. Sugar may be added while cooking if wished. Freezing apples as purée is quick and easy since they do not need to be peeled and cored. Simply chop, cook until soft and press through a sieve.

13

Blackberry

(Rubus fructicosus agg.)

Known as brambles, blackberries, or less familiarly, brumble-berries, this prized fruit can be found in abundance in early autumn, growing wild amongst the hips and haws in hedgerows heralding the advent of autumn. The nineteenth-century term, "blackberry summer" conjures up a picture of fine autumn days, when the blackberries are ready to be eaten.

Although smaller, firmer and frequently less accessible than cultivated varieties, wild blackberries have a more concentrated and superior flavour. Cuttings take well, and will grow successfully in most gardens provided the soil

is well-drained. Mid-autumn is the best month for planting; bury tips of cane shoots in soil and in the following spring, the established roots should bring forth new growth. Cut the old cane down to ground level and train the young canes along horizontal wires to facilitate easy picking the following year. This should render the blackberry picker's companion, the walking stick, obsolete! A little dug in compost will improve poor ground and since sunlight is

not a priority, site bushes in a slightly shaded area, leaving the sunny patches for those fruits which will really benefit from them. Cultivation has improved the berry size, the 'Merton Thornless' variety makes harvesting a less hazardous task and lengthens the season.

Blackberries, as with most soft fruits, are best eaten on the day when picked. but they do freeze well. Pick when ripened, that is when the fruit is plump, shiny and deep purple (matt reddish-purple coloured berries are over-ripe), and perfectly dry. Open freeze before packing in airtight containers. Unsuitable fruit can be frozen if cooked and sieved, but will keep for half as long—about six months. For bottling, choose large, ripe berries, discard stalks and any over-ripe fruit and proceed as for cherries.

Blackberries contain sufficient pectin to make excellently flavoured jellies (having too many pips for jam), and are the perfect companion for apple, combined in crumbles, pies, mousses or fools. Add to fruit compotes, sprinkle on cereal, purée, sieve and incorporate in ice cream or serve as a sauce to accompany poultry or game, alternatively make into a light, fruity red wine.

Blueberry

(Vaccinium family*)*

Often associated with their wild cousins (*Vaccinium mytrillus* also known as whortleberries, huckleberries or fruit of the moorland), some blueberries belong to the high bush type of *Vaccinium corymbosum*. It is this fruit which is sold in nurseries, particularly the 'Jersey' and 'Earliblue' varieties which bear larger berries than their wild counterparts. Shop bought berries are both scarce and dear so they are well worth cultivating.

Blueberries are relatively easy to grow, but it is a good idea to plant more than one variety to ensure adequate pollination takes place. If azaleas and rhododendrons flourish in your garden, so will blueberries which also thrive on a moist, acid soil. Enrich a light, sandy soil with peat and sawdust which curiously has an excellent effect on the shrub. It will grow well on relatively barren soil, which would be unsuitable for most other kinds of fruit, but requires plenty of sunshine so plant in a sunny situation sheltered from the wind.

Blueberry

19

The bell-shaped buds first appear in early spring and are deceptively hardy and resilient to frost. In midsummer the white blossom is succeeded by blue berries, similar in shape and size to cranberries (which are also of the *Vaccinium* group). The fruit hangs in decorative clusters from the branches and is covered with a white bloom, like the bloom found on plums. In the autumn the bushes become a blaze of marvellous colours—yellow, orange, gold and crimson, making the shrub prized both for its ornamental qualities as well as its produce.

Since the fruit is borne on the previous year's growth, and only on the thick branches, cut out any old or twiggy wood. This will also encourage growth from the base of the bush, keeping it trim and discouraging side shoots. Pest control can be minimal, although it is essential that some precaution, such as netting, is taken to safeguard the blueberries from the birds.

The time of harvesting varies slightly according to each variety, but the main season runs from midsummer to early autumn, each bush requiring four to five pickings.

Not all the fruit will ripen at once, so pick the berries individually, in order to segregate berry from stalk.

Blueberries have a slightly bitter, acidic taste. They can be eaten raw, with cream or yoghurt, or mixed with blackberries, currants, elderberries and damsons for a late summer fresh fruit salad. But they are best when cooked and sweetened to taste with a little lemon juice to heighten their flavour. To prepare: remove stalks and leaves, pick over and discard any undesirable berries, rinse and pat dry. Blueberry muffins are a traditional American favourite, and the fruit is also delicious in crumbles, pies, pancakes, gateaux or tarts.

Blueberries are a firm fruit so they keep fresh longer than other soft fruit, stored in the fridge they will last for three weeks. They also freeze well, either in syrup or dry packed, or can be bottled for use later in the year. Excess blueberries can be used for wine or jam, combine blueberry with raspberry or use spices, and add grated lemon rind and a cinnamon bark to the berries.

Cherry

(Sweet—*Prunus avium*,
sour—*Prunus cerasus*)

The sight of delicate pink and white cherry blossom, against azure spring skies with sheep and their newly born lambs grazing beneath, has inspired many an artist. The cherry tree belongs to the same family as apricots, peaches and plums and can be divided into two main categories; sweet and sour, the latter is self-fertilizing so ensures regular fruiting. Cherry trees favour chalky, well drained soil and a warm, but not hot, climate. The flowers appear early, making them vulnerable to severe spring frosts and cold winds which can ruin the chances of a good crop by destroying the blossom. Once ripe, precautions must be

taken to protect the fruit from predatory birds, and it is often worth the effort of training trees which can then be easily netted. During the last few days before maturity, cherries increase their weight by up to a third, so don't be tempted to pick until they are ready.

Whether delicate pink, creamy yellow, blood red, crimson or purple hue, whether round or heart-shaped, cherries are available in one form or another throughout the summer. Sweet cherries, such

21

as 'Black Heart', are usually eaten raw, but can also be cooked, whilst the acidic sour cherries (of which 'Morello' is the most widely known), are too tart to be eaten straight from the tree and are better suited for use in preserves. Sour cherry trees are smaller in stature and more convenient for garden cultivation, with the added advantage that birds tend to delay their feasting until the fruit is over-ripe. As with all stone fruit trees, any dead or badly positioned branches should be cut out after picking

since pruning during the autumn and winter encourages silver leaf disease. Cherry trees are also susceptible to canker.

Home grown cherries for use in puddings and preserves are a boon since bought ones are astronomically expensive. However, cherries do not keep well so eat within two to three days of picking. In times of glut, stone and poach the cherries in syrup until just soft, the liquid may then be thickened with a little arrowroot prior to use in pies (cherry meringue pie makes a novel alternative to lemon), flans, gateaux and pancakes, as a cheesecake topping or accompanying sauce for meats.

Black cherries make excellent jam, although their pectin content is low so it may be necessary to add a little acid in the form of lemon juice. The characteristics of sour 'Morello' cherries alter little with bottling. Pick when dry, selecting firm, ripe, blemish-free fruit, and take care to handle by the stalks to avoid bruising the cherries. Carefully remove the stalks, wash, and stone fruit if wished.

There are several methods for bottling fruit; the easiest and most satisfactory way is to pack the prepared cherries into clean, chip free, warmed jars. Add sufficient boiling water or syrup (using $\frac{1}{2}$lb (225g) sugar to 1 pint (600ml) water) to come within $\frac{3}{4}$in (2cm) of the jar's neck. Top with rubber rings and lids which have been scalded in boiling water. Stand the jars on baking trays lined with a couple of sheets of newspaper, and place in the middle of the oven set at 150°C, 300°F, Gas 2. Up to $4\frac{1}{2}$lb (2kg) of cherries, damsons, greengages, plums or rhubarb will take 40–50 minutes, allow longer for larger quantities. Apples, currants, berries and rhubarb which will subsequently be cooked, only take 30–40 minutes. Pears take longer, between 60–70 minutes. Screw tops or clips should then be fitted and the jars left for a day before making sure that they are properly sealed, if not, spoilage will soon set in. Remove screw top and if the jar can be lifted by its lid whilst maintaining the suction, it passes the test. Fruit from any unsealed jars must either be eaten within a couple of days or reprocessed. It is worth remembering that soft fruits, notably strawberries, raspberries and gooseberries do not bottle well, losing both colour and texture.

Both red and black cherries can be frozen, although the white varieties tend to discolour. Halve, stone and cover with sugar syrup to which a little lemon juice has been added to limit discoloration. This way the cherries will keep for up to a year. Defrost when out of season (they always seem twice as extravagant then!), and use as the basis for a fruit salad with bottled pears, a few bananas and melon sliced in, or add a little kirsch and serve with whipped cream.

Currants

(Ribes family*)*

Although of the same family and used in a similar way, red and white currants flourish under different growing conditions from black currants.

Black currants *(Ribes nigrum)* prefer heavier soils than red and white currants, but will grow reasonably well on all soil types (except chalk) which are well drained yet moist and fertile. Site in a sheltered location if possible. Since the fruit grows on new wood (as opposed to red and white currants which grow on the old spurs), annual pruning is essential; after harvesting the crop prune vigorously, right down to the base of the stems at ground level, thus ensuring new growth for the following year. Black currant bushes also benefit from a generous mulch. 'Laxton's Giant' is a good variety for gardens, although selection very much depends on the growing conditions and the desired time of fruition. The richness of this fruit as a source of vitamin C and its subsequent use as a treatment

for colds, has long been appreciated, the fruit being taken in the form of a syrup, cordial or as tea.

Red and white currants *(Ribes rubrum* and *Ribes album)* are grouped together since the white variety is very close to the red. Semi-transparent but without the red pigment, white currants are especially treasured because they rarely appear in the shops. A good supply of potash is necessary for bright coloured red currants and netting is essential in order to enjoy the bounty before our feathered friends have a chance! 'Red Lake' and 'Late White Grape' are two reputable varieties. Plant in sunny, sheltered situations where the risk of damage by frost is minimal. The bushes tend to last for a few years longer than black currants but for all currants some form of pest and disease control is required.

During the summer months clusters of the coloured fruit dangle beneath the plant's sheltering leaves, and as they reach maturity and ripen look fit to burst. Currants bruise easily so be careful to pick them by the strig rather than holding the fruit. Since their weight rapidly increases in the last few days before maturity, do not be tempted to pick until the berries are an evenly coloured deep black, red or creamy white, and soft but firm. They should be bright and glossy, any dull ones are past their best. Two to three picking sessions will often be necessary since not all the fruit will reach its peak at the same

brings out the flavour of black currants in sponge puddings whilst red currants combine well with other fruit, notably cherries and raspberries. Mix together for a refreshing summer flan, or use as a strudel filling with cream cheese. Currants make delicious hot or cold sauces, and when poached and sieved

time. Always pick during a dry spell since when wet they are susceptible to mildew.

Very ripe currants can be eaten raw, but because of their sharpness are usually stewed for use in pies, pancake fillings or cheesecake toppings. Cinnamon or mixed spice

can be used in mousses, soufflés and sorbets, try serving a scoop of each type of currant for a colourful effect. Blend currant juice (made from sieved over-ripe currants which have been simmered with sugar) with white wine and soda for a thirst

quenching drink on long, hot summer days. Currants have a high pectin content which makes them excellent for jellies and jams. When making jellies there is no need to strip the fruit from the strigs, for the basic method see Huntsman's Jelly (page 83).

Currants will keep for about a week in the fridge provided that any damaged fruit is removed but cover them to minimise shrinkage. Large,

firm, unsplit currants are suitable for bottling; remove the fruit from the strigs by holding the strig with one hand and gently running a fork down the fruit. Rinse and bottle as for cherries, but cook for less time. Alternatively open freeze raw, the currants can then be easily rubbed off the strigs before thawing. Over-ripe or hard fruit are best cooked. Add $\frac{1}{2}$ pint (300ml) of water to each 1lb (450g) of fruit, boil for 1 minute, strain through a jelly bag and dissolve $\frac{3}{4}$lb (350g) of sugar in each 1 pint (600ml) of juice. Poured into ice cube trays, this syrup may be frozen for six months, about half as long as whole currants. Use to flavour sparkling, fruity jellies or as a cordial.

Damson

(Prunus domestica ssp. insititia*)*

The hardiest member of the plum family, its name originates from an abbreviation of Damascene, 'the plum from Damascus', which was brought to this country during the Middle Ages by crusaders. To this day the small, sturdy trees have remained relatively uncultivated.

Damsons often grow in orchards or amongst hedgerows where they act as windbreaks for the more susceptible apple and pear trees or offer protection to farm animals. They are both attractive and functional, blossoming in the spring and providing pollen which will also benefit plums, if there is sufficient insect activity. Damson trees need little care apart from cutting out dead branches. Two well loved varieties are 'Merryweather', which has relatively large fruit most akin to a plum, but retains its distinct damson flavour, and 'Shropshire', widely grown in that county, which, although not a heavy cropper, has a good flavour. The main season runs from

late summer to mid autumn
and the fruit is ripe when it is
dark blue, verging on black,
and still fairly firm.

The smallness of damsons
makes them fiddly and time

consuming to prepare, so it is often more convenient to leave the fruit whole when using in pies and crumbles, or when a purée is needed to poach them in a little water until soft and then sieve to remove the stones. The pulp can be used for mousses, fools, jellies or wine making. Damson cheese, which is used like jam, is perhaps the most traditional recipe, ideal for when you have a glut on your hands. Cheeses use equal quantities of sugar to pulp, simmered together until thick, and are best kept for about a year to develop fully their flavour. Damsons also make excellent jam and, owing to their sharpness, are a good ingredient for chutneys, lending a sweet-sour taste to the relish (see page 84).

Pick the damsons and use within a couple of days since they do not keep for long. Freeze in heavy sugar syrup to which a little ascorbic acid powder, $\frac{1}{2}$ teaspoon (2.5ml spoon) to 1lb (450g) fruit, has been added, for up to eight months. Freeze unstoned (beware of their skins toughening as they age) or as a pulp for up to six months. Damsons also bottle well, remove the stalks, wipe and proceed as for cherries.

Elderberry

(Sambucus nigra)

Take a walk in any part of the countryside during autumn and you cannot fail to notice clusters of tiny round berries, bending the branches of the elder trees. The elderberry, which is technically a shrub, is native to Britain. Both the flowers and fruit of this wild plant can be put to good culinary use.

The attractive white flowers have long been appreciated as a fragrant flavouring, reminiscent of grapes, bound in muslin and infused with gooseberries (wonderful as jam) or rhubarb, the flowers impart a subtle change in flavour. Elderflowers also make a heady white wine with a delightful bouquet. For centuries apples were stored on a blanket of elderflowers, which gave them a delicate muscat aroma.

Sprays of ripened berries can be found during the autumn. Do not gather until they are plump and a really deep purple, green or red berries are under-ripe. Always go elderberry picking armed with a pair of scissors to cut off the main stalks just above each cluster. Use a fork to remove berries from strigs as you would for currants, and this way you will also avoid badly stained hands!

Elderberries may be frozen (follow directions for currants), made into preserves (see page 83 for Huntsman's Jelly), used as a syrup to flavour jellies, mixed with other berry fruit (sparingly as

their flavour is strong), or made into wine. Indeed elderberries have been called the 'Englishman's grape', such is their popularity for this purpose. Traditional country wine recipes, more often judged by potency rather than distinction of taste and clarity, have been passed down from generation to generation. Many connoisseurs have emerged as a result, all vowing that their particular nuances of method are superior. However, whether one takes wine-making seriously or just dabbles with it as a hobby, there are a few basic tips worth remembering: The fruit used should be fully ripened in order to ensure maximum flavour and colour. Any stalks and stones should be removed

to guard against bitterness. Elderberries, blackberries and sloes benefit from being heated to about 20°C, 70°F below boiling point for 15 minutes after crushing, and then being allowed to cool before straining. This extracts maximum colour and guards against bitterness which tends to occur if fermentation takes place on the pulp.

Elderberry wine should be kept for at least six months before serving. As a general rule, try to resist opening home made fruit wines until the following year, your patience will definitely be rewarded! During the winter, try serving elderberry wine heated with sugar, cinnamon, cloves and lemon peel for a warming mulled toddy.

Fig

(Ficus carica)

Introduced into this country by the Romans, fig trees have come a long way from their native Asia. They grow easily in our climate, although producing a crop is more difficult without the warmth and sunshine of the east to mature and ripen the fruit. Fig trees do better in the regions where winters are milder. Grow in a sheltered position on a south facing terrace or fan-trained (espalier) against a brick wall, so that the branches are fully exposed to the sun. Planting trees against a wall also serves to restrict root growth, particularly important in the case of figs since if the big tap root is allowed to grow unchecked it will reduce fruit yield. Fig trees prosper on remarkably poor soils but prefer a chalky, well drained sub-soil and plenty of water during the growing season. Ripe figs are a common sight abroad, since the trees bear three crops annually. However, in colder climes trees grown outdoors yield one harvest, with the fruits beginning to show in late

spring and lasting until the autumn frosts. Figs should be left to ripen on the tree to ensure good flavour, and as anyone who has grown them will know, taste best freshly picked when still warm from the sun. A drop of nectar seen in the 'eye' at the base of the fig is an indication that it is ready for eating. Ripened figs are very soft and should be eaten straight away.

There are few varieties of figs, and these are usually divided into two groups, green or purple skinned. The best known varieties are 'Breba' which has a green skin, yellow flesh and pink seeds, and the prevalent 'Brown Turkey' which is a large, pear-shaped fig, purple/brown in colour. 'White Ischia' is a good strain for wall culture.

Figs have a subtle flavour but are sweet and therefore valued in their dried form in cakes, steamed puddings and pastries, or gently poached with a little mixed spice. Drying is one of the oldest methods of preservation and certainly the most natural. Unfortunately the climate is not always ideal for following the traditional method for drying figs in the sun. A very low oven, airing cupboard or warming trolley, anywhere

where the temperature is about 50°C (120°F) and does not exceed 70°C (160°F), with freely circulating air are the alternatives. The process takes three to four days if drying conditions are maintained for half-day periods at a time. When the figs are thoroughly dried they should have shrivelled and become firm. Try squeezing, if any juice runs out then continue drying for a little longer. A cooling rack covered with muslin provides a good surface on which to lay the fruit. Make sure that the figs do not touch, and turn over twice a day. Leave at room temperature

38

for a couple of days after
drying before packing in an
airtight container. Dried fruit
should keep for a year and
can be reconstituted by
soaking in water, or natural
fruit juice, overnight.

Gooseberry

(Ribes grossularia)

Gooseberries have always been surrounded by superstition. In the past they were quaintly called feaberries, due to folklore belief that in the face of danger fairies would take refuge in the bushes since the prickles would protect them from their pursuers.

Rivalry amongst fellow countrymen to produce better and larger varieties was once rife. As a consequence of this zealous cross-breeding we now have many varieties to choose from—yellow, green, red and white, smooth or hairy, dessert or cooking, many of which were named after breeder, statesmen or royalty.

Gooseberries flourish in this country, even preferring the cooler parts, and grow on most soils, but despite being relatively hardy they should be kept clear of frost pockets. The first berries ripen in late spring and by planting several varieties, harvesting can continue until early autumn. Pruning, to open the centre of the bush so that it receives maximum sunlight for ripening and facilitates picking, should be done as

41

soon as the year's harvest has been reaped. Not all the berries will be ready at once so two to three pickings may be required. If the gooseberries are to be eaten raw, ensure that they are really ripe, just soft to the touch, plump and slightly yellow or pale red wine coloured according to the variety. 'Careless' is a popular garden strain for cooking and preserving whereas 'Whinam's Industry', a dark red dessert variety, is an excellent choice since eating gooseberries are rarely available in the shops.

Gooseberries make a delicious crumble (mix some chopped hazelnuts into the crumble mixture) hold their shape well in pies, flans and sponge puddings and are an excellent accompaniment to fish such as mackerel. Poached and sieved they can be incorporated into fools, mousses and ice cream, and have the advantage of not needing topping and tailing if prepared in this way. They contain a good proportion of pectin so are ideal for jam—try mixing with strawberries for a change. Any small, hard berries can be cooked and the pulp used to make wine. 'Careless' and 'Leveller' make particularly good table wine.

This fruit keeps well in the fridge for about three weeks, provided all over-ripe specimens are removed. Cooking gooseberries freeze better, although dessert varieties are also suitable if under-ripe. As with all fruit, pick and freeze immediately to ensure that as few nutrients as possible are lost. Dry packing is a perfectly satisfactory and easy method, which also makes topping and tailing quicker—just rub off the ends when still frozen. Stewed and puréed fruit freezes for half as long as whole gooseberries, about six months.

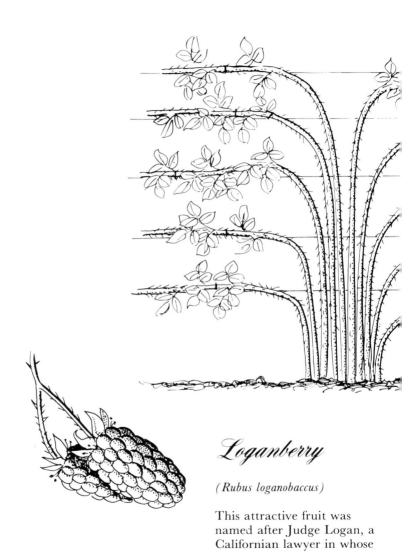

Loganberry

(Rubus loganobaccus)

This attractive fruit was
named after Judge Logan, a
Californian lawyer in whose
garden the first cross between
a raspberry and

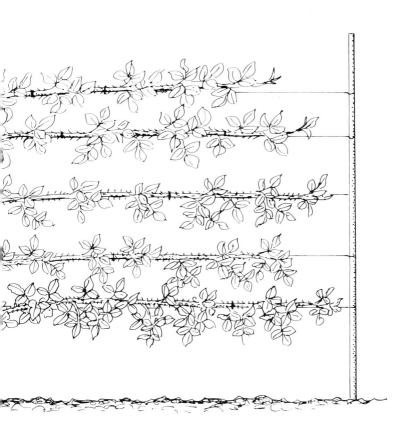

blackberry/dewberry hybrid was said to have occurred. This led to the cultivation of thornless varieties. Loganberry plants are fairly hardy and grow like blackberries, although the canes need some form of support, usually a wire fence or meshing. If the plants are well drained and have a plentiful supply of nitrogen, a generous harvest should be forthcoming. The large, elongated berries are a muted deep red/purple colour and ripen in late summer. Since they are more acidic than either raspberries or blackberries they can only be eaten raw when fully ripe,

that is when they are very juicy and the plugs come out easily. Since the fruit is borne on new canes each year, pruning is vital. Once the fruit has been picked, cut out the old canes and tie in the new as for blackberries.

Pick and use on the same day since the berries only keep in the fridge for a day. They can be frozen in the same way as raspberries but firm, deep red fruit are perfect for bottling. Remove the stalks and proceed as for cherries but cook for 15–20 minutes less. They are excellent in any dishes where raspberries or blackberries are called for, just add a little more sugar to taste. If you have a large enough crop make loganberry jam, which is always a little bit special and a real treat for spooning on to scones with lashings of thick cream. Use

firm fruit as bruised or over-ripe berries will not set as well. To make loganberry jam place equal quantities of fruit and sugar in a pan and heat gently until the sugar dissolves, bring to the boil and heat until setting point is reached (see Huntsman's Jelly, page 83 for testing procedure), stirring occasionally to prevent burning. Pot and seal as for Damson Chutney (page 84).

46

Mulberry

(Morus nigra)

Mulberry trees enjoyed popularity in the early seventeenth century during the reign of King James I, and Buckingham Palace was built on the site of James's mulberry orchard. Many of the trees in England today date back to this period. Explorers of the time had witnessed silkworms living off mulberry trees in China, and since the King felt that it would be beneficial to encourage the growth of a silk industry in this country, arrangements for the introduction of these trees into Britain were made. Unfortunately the explorers' observations of silkworm habits seem to have been somewhat limited as they brought back the black variety, *Morus nigra* (which bears edible fruit) rather than the white sister tree, *Morus alba* (which silkworms feed on). Britain never became famous for its thriving silk industry, but gained a very attractive addition to the garden instead!

The trees live to a ripe old age, yielding improved fruit with the passing of years, but require increasing attention in the form of some kind of support since their wood is relatively soft. Preferring sandy soil and a sunny situation, mulberries blossom very late, thus contriving to escape the effects of crippling frosts. The trees are often found in a prominent position, like the middle of the lawn for two excellent reasons: firstly they provide an ornamental centre piece, and secondly the fruit is only ready for eating when it is fully ripened and has fallen to the ground—thus the grass cushions their fall and makes gathering easier.

The main difficulty is in harvesting the succulent crop before the birds do, some form of netting is therefore advisable during late summer and early autumn when the berries mature to a deep crimson.

The mulberry tree is undemanding. Any odd, mis-shapen or dead branches must be cut out, but otherwise it is rarely troubled by disease or pests. A peculiar, but intriguing characteristic of this tree lies in the shape of the leaves. These are difficult to define since they vary not only from tree to tree, but to the extent that leaves on the top branches differ from those on the bottom of the same tree.

Mulberries are similar to loganberries in appearance and flavour, although they are slightly more acidic. Excellent when bottled (follow method for loganberries), they can be used, sweetened, in fruit flans, jams, or for wine making. Make a delicious wild berry compote with blackberries; poach both types of berry in a little sugar syrup to which a stick of cinnamon and pared strip of lemon rind has been added, and spoon over steamed sponge pudding as a prelude to warming winter puddings.

Pear

(Pyrus communis)

Pears are one of our most underrated fruits. Enjoyed at their prime they should be sweet, fragrant and juicy with soft, creamy coloured flesh. The risk of disappointment lies in incorrect ripening techniques which lead to a gritty textured and poorly flavoured pear.

The fruit's blossom appears early and in consequence is vulnerable to frosts since the bloom is sensitive. Sheltered conditions are thus preferable and pear trees flourish in

walled gardens or if grown against a wooden fence. Many varieties are self-sterile so more than one kind of tree may have to be grown in order to ensure that fruit is produced. Fairly rich, heavy soil which retains water during periods of dry weather is ideal. Once the fruit has set, thinning is often necessary to ensure a good quality crop of medium, even-sized fruits. However, nature usually attends to this herself and the tree will naturally shed most of its unwanted pears rendering human intervention minimal. Pears are ready for picking from midsummer but autumn pears picked at the perfect moment are better for storing.

Harvesting is as much of an art as the cultivation since the fruit should not be allowed to ripen on the tree, as this results in a gritty texture. The temptation is to leave the pears for just a couple of days more, which will be too long. Conversely, under-ripe pears do not store well as after a while the flesh dries out. The secret then is to catch the fruit when it has matured but not yet reached the ripened stage. Maturity can be measured by the ease with which the stalks part from the branch. Gently cup the palm of your hand under the pear (gripping will

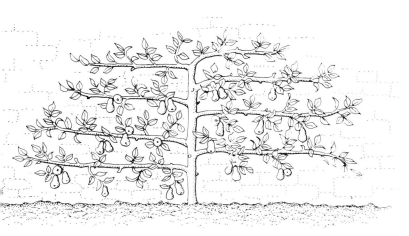

'Comice'

'Conference'

'Williams'

cause bruising) and lift upwards. If the fruit is ready for picking it will come away easily. Pears will then ripen in two to three days in a warm environment. If they are to be stored for use later in the year it is necessary to choose a cool site. Ripening itself is denoted by a softening of the fruit which yields slightly when gently pressed, this softening is sometimes accompanied by a yellowing of the skin which may also become flushed with red. Store as for apples, checking frequently and picking out any fruit which are ripe for eating.

Pears are also akin to apples in that there are both cooking and eating varieties, the former being particularly suited to the north whilst dessert pears need the warmth of the south to maximize their flavour. Popular cooking pears include 'Vicar of Winkfield' and 'King Edward', whilst 'Doyenne du Comice' is an excellent dessert variety. 'Conference', named after the International Pear Conference of 1885 where it distinguished itself, combines the best of both worlds as it is excellent both cooked and uncooked. Indeed most eating pears can be cooked, their flavour combines particularly well with coffee and chocolate. Use fresh pears in a pastry flan

case arranged on mocha-flavoured confectioners' custard. Incorporate pears into fruit salads or serve as an unusual starter by coring and piling a blue cheese, chive and walnut filling into the cavity. Pears can also be used in making soups. Should the pears have a disappointing flavour, poach them in wine, cider or a ginger-flavoured syrup, either in the oven or on the hob—there is nothing quite like mulled wine pears to lift dampened spirits on a dreary winter's night. Alternatively, where a chutney recipe calls for apples, pears will do equally well, although the set may not be as good since pears have a low pectin level.

Freezing is not usually recommended as the fruit tends to lose its subtle flavour. Once cut, surfaces brown readily as with applies and on thawing their texture suffers. However,if peeled, halved, cored and poached in syrup they will keep for eight months. A little added ascorbic acid, $\frac{1}{4}$ teaspoon (1.25ml spoon) to 1 pint (600ml) syrup, helps to limit discoloration. Pears do bottle well; choose just ripe fruit, peel, halve and core. Dip in brine and rinse just before packing (see cherries for method). Cooking pears are usually stewed in sugar syrup until just tender before packing. Skinned, cored and quartered pears can be successfully dried following the same procedure as for figs. Another method of preservation is in the form of 'perry', the pear equivalent of cider, which is made by leaving the juice of ripe pears to ferment and adding sugar to heighten its alcohol content. Traditionally specific varieties—such as 'Thorn', 'Butt' and 'Red Pear' were cultivated for this rather potent end.

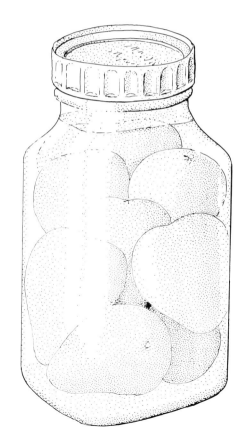

'Pershore Eg[g]'

'Cherry Plum'

'Blue Stanley'

'Victoria'

58

Plum

(Prunus domestica)

Gage

(Prunus italica)

Many varieties, different in appearance and taste, belong to the same family—*prunus*. Sloes and bullaces are often found growing wild, and are almost unrecognizable as belonging to the plum species.

Sloes are particularly popular for use in flavouring gin. They are deep violet in colour, whereas other members of the family, greengages, are yellow/green, with a delectable, sweet and slightly scented flavour, such is the diversity of this group. Initially the greengage was known in britain by its French name, 'Reine Claude' in deference to the French Queen, but on subsequent introduction to England adopted the name of its introducer, Sir Thomas Gage.

'Greengage'

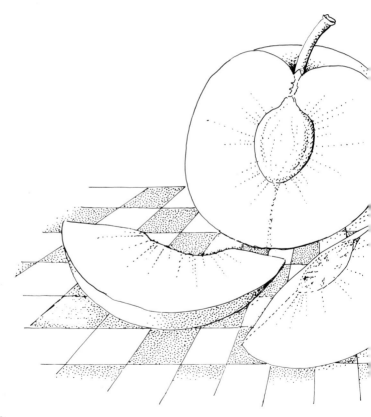

Similarly, the Czar plum was so called to flatter a visiting Russian Emperor of the time.

Plum trees prefer a heavy, well drained, lime-rich soil (although gages do better on lighter ground) and require some protection from the wind. Dead wood should be cut out but pruning is really only necessary where the tree is grown on a wall terrace, a position particularly favoured by gages. Thinning is a must. Although at the time it may seem a waste of fruit, it is necessary to restrict heavily covered trees since nature has an inbuilt regulatory system and if a tree is over-burdened with fruit one year the next year's crop will be correspondingly poor. In order to balance this tendency towards glut followed by fruitless years it is necessary to thin the immature fruit by hand after any likely candidates have dropped naturally.

The plums must be fully matured and ripe before picking. If the stalk comes away easily from the branch, the fruit feels soft and has its characteristic colour, whether purple, crimson, green or yellow, then the moment is right. As with all fruit, pick when dry. Any imperfect specimens which have been deliberately by-passed during harvesting should afterwards be picked and thrown on to the compost heap, since deteriorating fruit can damage the tree. According to variety, plums are available from midsummer to mid-autumn but the gage season is somewhat shorter. The 'Victoria' plum is a classic, of good size and a 'sure cropper', it is a dependable favourite for garden cultivation. Both dessert—such as the small, sweet 'Early Laxton' variety, and cooking plums, 'Pershore Yellow Egg' for instance, which are rather more acidic and drier, may be grown. If

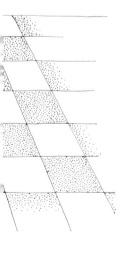

you have limited space, then a dessert plum tree is probably more suitable since cookers tend to be larger, but dessert trees do need more shelter. Dessert plums when ripe are refreshing eaten raw, but on the whole plums are usually stewed or cooked in some way before serving. They make excellent crumbles, particularly the purple/maroon varieties, and are good in sponge puddings, served with yoghurt and muesli as a layered pudding, or made into a sauce laced with rum. Greengages, white grapes and apricots, doused with a liqueur syrup make a delicious summer compote, or poached, the gages can be combined with almond flavoured confectioners' custard for a choux pastry filling. Plums make superb chutney, or better still, jam, if you have so many you don't know what to do with them. The lovely thing about plum jam is that it may be green, red or crimson according to the variety used. Cooking plums are better suited to jam making because they naturally contain a higher percentage of acid and so give a better set, as do slightly under-ripe fruit.

Both cooking and eating plums freeze well. Halve,

remove stones and freeze in sugar syrup with a little added lemon juice to preserve the colour. Whole fruit can be frozen but the stones tend to taint the flesh with a slightly almondy flavour after about six months. This flavour exudes from the kernels inside the stone, which can easily be removed and added to poached plums, pies or jam to lend a subtle flavour.

Other forms of preservation include pickling in a sugar and vinegar solution with added spices. Damsons are also delicious served in this way with cold meats or, more

62

unusually, used to garnish pizzas for a sweet-sour flavour. Plums can be successfully bottled (following the method for cherries) for which the purple varieties, when they are still red and unripe, are best. They also respond well to drying, particularly the late varieties. Use dark-skinned types and dry as for figs. Mis-shapen or split plums are excellent for wine making. Keep the finest plums until Christmas by following the old fashioned and cheering custom of steeping in brandy!

Quince

(Cydonia oblonga)

Traditionally referred to as the "Golden Apple" of centuries past, quinces were symbolic of love, happiness and fertility, hence their inclusion in Roman wedding feasts. Nowadays they are less widely grown, the squat trees/shrubs, which live to a ripe old age, tend to be found near ponds, streams and marshland where they thrive on the moist conditions. The ancient, twisted trees are full of character and flourish in the warmth of the south since they rely on sunlight to ripen the fruit. Grow in a situation which is sheltered from the wind, ideally trained against a wall or fence. Quince trees require minimal attention, just remove any dead or overcrowded branches.

There are many varieties, *Chaenomele speciosa* or the Japanese quince is best known. The fruit may broadly be divided into apple or pear-shaped and should not be picked until late autumn and then left to ripen in store. The pear-shaped quinces keep best. Lay them out on paper or straw so that they are not touching, and leave until they have turned from green to yellow, which may take two to three months. Even when ripened, the fruit will be hard and acidic and requires cooking before serving.

In spite of their mundane apperance, quinces are the Cinderella of fruits having a strong fragrant aroma, delectable flavour and subtle

colour when cooked. In the past they were cut in half and arranged around rooms as air fresheners. It is therefore wise to store them well away from other foods which may be likely to absorb the strong smell. Although too gritty in texture and scent to be consumed on their own, quinces provide a resourceful secret ingredient for home cooking, combining particularly well with apples. Use one quince to six cooking apples for pies and crumbles and notice the difference. Quince jelly is the pride and joy of every fruit grower and cook alike. Cooking them is like watching the frog turn into Prince Charming. There's no need to peel and core the quinces; wash, roughly chop,

cook and you'll see the flesh change from cream to a beautiful salmon pink. Quince jelly is an ideal accompaniment for cold meat such as game and lamb. But the main use for quinces is as a preserve which is fitting since they were the initial basic ingredient of marmalade—*marmelo* being Portuguese for quince.

Raspberry

(Rubus idaeus)

Small, wine coloured wild raspberries are a familiar sight in the north during summertime, growing on hilly terrain with acidic soil which provides ideal conditions for this hardy plant. Raspberries were also known as hindberries in the past and it is only through cultivation over the years that the raspberry as we know it today, larger and juicier, has emerged. The fruit is available, according to variety, from midsummer to mid-autumn. Healthy canes should be carefully planted in late autumn on well drained soil in rows running north to south. In a sunny, yet sheltered position, the canes should fruit in their second year. Once shoots are a good length, tie to supports to prevent them breaking, doing so will also make picking much easier. One drawback with raspberries is that they are notoriously prone to infestation by pests and spraying is often necessary. The old, darker coloured canes can be cut back to ground level the moment the last of the fruit has been gathered. This should be

thorough in order that sufficient new cane is produced for the following year's fruit. The berries are ready for picking when they are evenly coloured and come away easily leaving the plug behind. Several pickings are often required and any mouldy fruit should be removed from the canes since when over-ripe they are liable to become plagued with grey mould fungus which spreads over the entire crop. 'Lloyd George', a New Zealand strain, is an excellent choice, it often yields two crops—one in summer and the other during autumn ,and the berries are of a good flavour. 'Malling Jewel' and

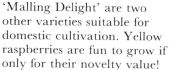

'Malling Delight' are two other varieties suitable for domestic cultivation. Yellow raspberries are fun to grow if only for their novelty value!

Ideally raspberries should be picked and eaten while still warm from the sun, sprinkled with a little sugar, to bring out their flavour, and covered with cream. If the berries must be kept for any time, store in a cool place. Freshly picked raspberries surpass all other fruits in their quality of flavour—the difference is impossible to describe as the pleasure must be personally experienced! Arrange in pastry cases, fold into cream for a gateau, *millefeuille* or roulade filling or pile into meringue baskets. Purée for sauces to serve with pancakes, or combine with cream and freeze. Slightly under-ripe raspberries also make excellent jam (although rather pippy and of low pectin content so try combining with apples).

If you are lucky enough to have a glut of raspberries then freezing is probably the simplest and most useful way of preserving them since they respond to this treatment very well, still retaining their colour, flavour and shape for up to a year. Make sure that you choose the best samples,

69

those which are just ripe, and that they are dry since damp fruit goes mouldy quickly. Hull and open freeze unwashed fruit and pack into rigid containers. The berries are best defrosted by spreading out in a single layer and allowing to thaw overnight in the fridge. Any over-ripe berries which are to be frozen should be pulped and used within six months.

Preserving in alcohol is an

old-fashioned method which has recently found new popularity. Special jars, of German/Austrian origin known as *rumtopfs* are now generally available, but any large, wide-necked jar with a fitted lid will do. Layer all manner of soft fruit with an equal weight of caster sugar, adding to the jar as you harvest the different types, and topping up with rum each time so that the fruit is submerged (the liquor prevents the fruit from fermenting). To ensure that the fruit does not rise and become exposed to the atmosphere, it may be necessary to use a saucer to weight it down. Small fruit—berries, currants, gooseberries and cherries can be added whole, but it is best to slice larger ones, such as apples and pears. Quartered plums soak up the flavour of rum well, and you may like to fill a *rumtopf* with this fruit alone. Christmas is a good time to indulge in this heady concoction; spoon fruit and juices on to plain steamed puddings, use to liven up ice cream or home made custard sauce. Any remaining liquor should be filtered, bottled and left to mature for two to three months before being opened.

Rhubarb

(Rheum rhabarbarum)

Although used in this country as a fruit, botanically speaking rhubarb is a vegetable, and abroad is served as such, unsweetened, as an accompaniment to a main course. The name rhubarb is

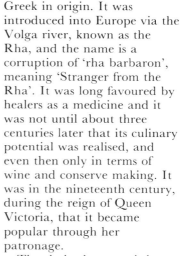

Greek in origin. It was introduced into Europe via the Volga river, known as the Rha, and the name is a corruption of 'rha barbaron', meaning 'Stranger from the Rha'. It was long favoured by healers as a medicine and it was not until about three centuries later that its culinary potential was realised, and even then only in terms of wine and conserve making. It was in the nineteenth century, during the reign of Queen Victoria, that it became popular through her patronage.

The rhubarb season is long, running from mid-spring to late autumn, and 'forcing' permits an even earlier crop. It is tolerant of most conditions although it prefers a south-facing bank where it receives maximum sunshine. To obtain early rhubarb the plants must be covered with manure and grown either under glass or an upended earthenware pot, which acts as an insulator and raises the temperature. This early, forced rhubarb tends to have pale pink, thin stalks, whereas rhubarb which has been grown outside may be deep pink or green in colour and has a stronger flavour. As the plant matures so its acidity increases and the stalks become fibrous and sometimes need stringing before use. It is therefore best to harvest rhubarb while it is still young and tender and preserve in one of the following ways for later use:

Rhubarb freezes well, retaining its colour and flavour, although it does tend to collapse on thawing since it has a high water content. Discard leaves, which are poisonous, trim end, slice stalk into 1in (2.5cm) lengths, wash and pat dry. The rhubarb can then be frozen in a container for three to four months. If blanched for 1 minute and frozen in a sugar syrup it will keep for up to a year. Pulped rhubarb takes up less room and is an excellent standby for fruit fool, quick and simple to make it requires very few ingredients, but is delicious all the same.

Spring is the best time for bottling rhubarb when the tenderness of the young, pink stalks can be captured. It is best to shrink the fruit first. Wash and cut into lengths, pour on hot syrup and leave overnight, then pack into jars, cover with syrup and proceed as for cherries. Old rhubarb need not be wasted and can be made into jam or ginger and rhubarb chutney. Its pectin level is low, so add a few apples to make sure that the preserve sets.

If you do find that you have picked too much to eat at once, but not enough to warrant freezing, the rhubarb will keep for a couple of days in a cool, dry, dark place. Should it become limp a useful refreshing tip is to treat as for flowers; stand the stalks in a jug of water for about an hour and after a good drink they should be revitalized! Rhubarb's acidity makes cooking essential, poach gently with sugar in a little water, be careful not to overcook since it will quickly lose its shape and disintegrate. Rhubarb combines particularly well with ginger and orange since they counteract this acidity, and also has an affinity with rose water. Add these flavourings to heighten its taste in pies, flans, upside down sponge puddings and charlottes.

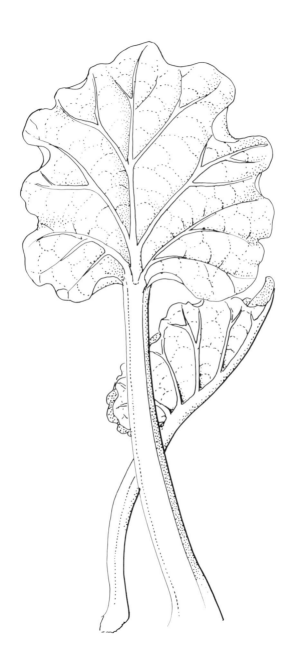

Strawberry

(Fragaria ananassa)

Strawberries differ from most other fruits in having their seeds embedded in the outside skin rather than contained within the berry. Like raspberries, they have evolved from miniature wild varieties, subsequently bred from American species to achieve the larger, less seedy, juicy-fleshed strawberry of today. However, wild, or their cultivated counterparts, Alpine strawberries can still be found

and they provide the perfect decoration for a host of puddings.

Fertile, fairly heavy soils are most suitable for strawberry growing, chalky ground should be avoided. Their growth pattern is such that the plants are very near to the ground making them vulnerable to frost damage which results in blackened flower centres. As protection against frosts during blossoming, and to keep the fruit clean, the plants are surrounded with straw or black plastic film. Choose a raised site in a sunny position to encourage ripening.

Generous manuring and watering in dry weather will help to produce a first-class crop. Although typically regarded as a delight of summer picnics and tea parties, strawberries may fruit from midsummer to late autumn, or yield both a summer and an autumn crop, according to the variety. 'Cambridge Favourite' is a summer cropper while 'Gento' is autumn fruiting. Since strawberries are particularly prone to pests the use of pesticide is often necessary.

Once one or two of the berries are ripe, that is evenly red, the plants need picking over each day to ensure that there is no wastage through spoilage, as the strawberries ripen very quickly, particularly in warm, sunny weather. Do not pick when wet and if they are to be kept for a couple of days before eating store in a cool place with their plugs intact. Similarly, if the berries need washing, do so just before serving and do not remove plugs, otherwise the cavity will be filled with water and the fruit's texture spoiled.

Since biblical times strawberries have been associated with goodness and purity, mainly because of their shape and, as opposed to other berries, their lack of thorns. It is therefore fitting that they are best enjoyed unadulterated, dipped into sugar and covered with cream. They are one of our most versatile fruits, giving a colourful finish to many puddings. Arrange on a bed of cream in delicate meringue baskets, in pastry or sponge cases, or dip the ends into bitter chocolate and serve as sweets. The fruit will purée easily, just push through a sieve and use in ice creams, sorbets, jellies, mousses, cheesecakes and sauces for steamed puddings, ice cream and pancakes. Strawberries can be poached but tend to lose their colour and shape on heating.

It is always surprising that home-made strawberry jam remains a favourite since the berries have a poor pectin content making it necessary to add either lemon juice or commercial pectin to obtain a good set. For a more natural preserve, the juice of a high pectin fruit such as redcurrant or gooseberry can be used.

The main advantage of making your own jam, apart from excellence of flavour, is the opportunity to experiment with the fruits available at

your fingertips. To produce interesting combinations—try strawberry and greengage, or a mixed berry concoction. Home-made jams are perfect as gifts. To ensure the preserve looks really professional, allow it to cool in the pan before ladling into jars, since this will prevent any whole fruit from floating to the top.

Whole strawberries freeze notoriously badly, losing their colour, flavour and texture. However, by choosing small, barely ripened fruit, open freezing and finally thawing in the fridge, acceptable results can be achieved. Freezing as a purée does not cause as many problems. Add a little sugar and lemon juice before freezing and you have a supply at hand until the following year's harvest.

Gooseberry Flapjack Cheesecake

Serves 10

2oz (50g) butter/margarine
2oz (50g) soft light brown sugar
2 tablesps (2 × 15ml spoons) golden syrup
4oz (125g) rolled oats
1lb (450g) gooseberries topped and tailed

4oz (125g) caster sugar
2 tablesps (2 × 15ml spoons) water
0.4oz (11g) sachet powdered gelatine
4oz (125g) cream cheese
4oz (125g) cottage cheese, sieved
$\frac{1}{4}$ pint (150ml) double cream, whipped

Warm together butter, brown sugar and golden syrup, without boiling, until melted. Stir in oats and press into base of a greased 8in (20cm) round, loose-bottomed cake tin. Bake at 160°C, 325°F, Gas 3, for 25 minutes until golden. Cool.

Place gooseberries and sugar in a pan, cover and poach for 10–15 minutes until just soft. Cool, purée and sieve. Sprinkle gelatine on to the measured water and dissolve by steaming over a pan of hot water. Cool slightly and whisk into gooseberry purée. Beat cheeses until smooth and gradually add gooseberry mixture. Fold in cream and pour over flapjack base. Shake to level surface. Refrigerate until set. Decorate with piped cream.

Frosted gooseberries make an attractive finish for this cheesecake, simply brush fruit with a little lightly beaten egg white, dust thickly with caster sugar and leave to dry. Shake off excess sugar before arranging on cheesecake. Fruits with a skin, such as currants, blueberries and cherries can also be sugared. For a change, use one of these fruits in the cheesecake instead of gooseberries.

Huntsman's Jelly

**Makes approximately
4lb (1.8kg)**

2lb (900g) crab apples, washed
and roughly chopped

1lb (450g) blackberries
1lb (450g) stripped elderberries
2 pints (1.2 litres) water
2lb (900g) approximately granulated sugar

Place apples, blackberries and elderberries in a large pan. Add
water and simmer gently, uncovered, for about 1 hour until the
fruit has softened and is pulpy. Press with the back of a spoon to
mash fruit. Scald a jelly/muslin bag with boiling water. Pour in fruit
mixture and leave to strain for about 1 hour, until all the liquid has
dripped through. Do not squeeze the bag since this will cloud the
jelly.

Measure juice and to each pint (600ml) add 1lb (450g) sugar.
(This recipe yields about 2 pints (1.2 litres).) Dissolve sugar in
liquid, bring to the boil and boil rapidly for 15–20 minutes until
setting point is reached. To test if the jelly has reached setting point,
place a little on a saucer and when cool if a skin has formed, the jelly
is ready. Skim off any scum and pot as for damson chutney.

This recipe combines three wild fruits from the hedgerows—soft,
pinky-red crab apples and deep purple elderberries and blackberries—reminiscent of pink and black huntsmen's coats. Quinces,
redcurrants and crab apples are renowned for the subtly coloured
and delicately flavoured jellies which they yield, whilst more
unusual combinations between familiar fruits include apple and
pear, plum and ginger and gooseberry and greengage.

Damson Chutney

Makes approximately 4lb (1.8kg)

2lb (900g) damsons, washed and with the stalks removed
1lb (450g) cooking apples, peeled, cored and roughly chopped
1lb (450g) onions, peeled and roughly chopped

1 pint (600ml) red wine vinegar
1 teasp (5 ml spoon) ground ginger
1 teasp (5 ml spoon) salt
1 teasp (5ml spoon) ground allspice
$\frac{1}{2}$ teasp (2.5ml spoon) cayenne pepper
12oz (350g) granulated sugar

Place all ingredients, except sugar, in a large, uncovered pan and simmer for about 45 minutes until fruit and onion are softened. Stir in sugar and simmer for another 45 minutes until thick and pulpy, scooping off damson stones as they rise to the surface. Stir occasionally. Chutney is ready if no liquid runs out of the mixture when a little is cooled on a plate.

Pour into clean, dry, warm jars. Place a waxed circle on top, wipe rim with a clean cloth and cap with a non-metallic screw-on lid. Cool, wipe jars and label.

Plums may be used in place of damsons in this recipe. Apples and rhubarb also make good chutney.

Orchard Lattice Torte

Serves 10

4oz (125g) sultanas
2 tablesps (2 × 15ml spoons) calvados
4oz (125g) butter/margarine
5oz (150g) caster sugar
6oz (175g) self-raising flour
1 egg, beaten
1 teasp (5ml spoon) cinnamon
1½lb (700g) cooking apples

Soak sultanas in calvados overnight.

Cream butter with 2oz (50g) sugar until light and fluffy. Beat in flour with enough egg to make a stiff, manageable dough. Wrap and chill for at least an hour.

Mix remaining sugar with cinnamon. Peel, core and thinly slice apples. Combine with sugar and add sultanas.

Press two-thirds of the pastry evenly into base and halfway up the sides of an 8in (20cm) spring-clip round cake tin. Pack apple mixture into pastry case. Roll out remaining dough on a lightly floured surface and cut into thin strips. Lay across the flan in a lattice pattern. Brush with remaining egg and bake at 180°C, 350°F, Gas 4 for 1 hour 10 minutes. Serve warm or cold with a dollop of thick cream.

A sophisticated version of our traditional apple pie, this is a Continental-style recipe made with a rich pastry. The calvados imparts a delightfully mysterious aroma and flavour.

Summer Pudding

Serves 6–8

1lb (450g) black/red/white currants
4oz (125g) caster sugar
2 tablesps (2 × 15ml spoons) water
8oz (225g) raspberries
6–7 × ½in (12.5mm) thick slices bread from a day-old, large white sandwich loaf

Place currants, sugar and water in a pan, cover and poach for about 10 minutes until fruit is soft but still holds its shape. Stir in raspberries and leave to cool.

Trim crusts from bread cut to line a 1½ pint (900ml) pudding basin, fitting closely to avoid any gaps. Keep 1½ slices for the lid. Spoon fruit and juice into lined basin, reserving a little juice. Cover with remaining bread. Place a saucer, which just fits inside basin, on top and weigh down. Leave in a cool place overnight. Carefully turn out from the mould and spoon reserved juice over any unsoaked bread. Decorate with fresh raspberries and sprigs of currants and serve with a blend of sweetened whipped cream and yoghurt.

Use whatever fresh soft fruits happen to be in season—cherries, strawberries, and gooseberries are equally delicious, or why not make an autumn pudding with pears, blueberries and blackberries!

National Trust
Fruit Gardens to Visit

Acorn Bank
Cumbria

Baddesley Clinton
Warwickshire

Barrington Court
Somerset

Bateman's
East Sussex

Calke Abbey
Derbyshire

Canons Ashby
Northants

Chartwell
Kent

Cotehele
Cornwall

Erddig
Clwyd

Gunby Hall
Lincolnshire

Ham House
Surrey

Hardwick Hall
Derbyshire

Hezlett House
County Londonderry

Hidcote Manor Gardens
Gloucestershire

Nunnington Hall
Yorkshire

Peckover House
Cambridgeshire

Powis Castle
Powys

Trerice
Cornwall

Upton House
Warwickshire

Wallington
Northumbria

Westbury Court Gardens
Gloucestershire

Wordsworth House
Cumbria